Contents

Reflections of the statue of Mercury and the Hall Tower among the lilies. ⤴

The Christ Church crest on the Hall stairs vault. ⤴

Coloured light streaming from the cathedral's St Frideswide window. ⤴

Tom Tower stands majestically above the main entrance to Christ Church on St Aldates. ⤵

1 Introduction by Jan Morris

A Victorian cartoon shows an American tourist making an inquiry at the Porters' Lodge of Christ Church, Oxford, in those days unquestionably the most pompous among the constituent colleges of Oxford University. "Say", he demands of the functionary inside, "is this purely an educational establishment, or can we get a snack here?"

The bowler-hatted porter probably gave him a dusty answer, but it was a forgivable request, and might easily be made at the Porters' Lodge today (where the gentleman – or lady – on duty still wears a bowler hat, but is called in new-speak a Custodian). Christ Church has indeed been one of England's prime educational establishments for almost 500 years, and is now a progressively modern college in a very modern university. But it is much more than that, too.

It is the seat of a cathedral, for one thing. It is an architectural exhibition. It is a treasure house and a portrait gallery. It is a place of literature and beautiful music. It is a school of statesmen, eminent divines, men and women prominent in all walks of life. It is a legend and a myth. "Sir", Dr Johnson once proclaimed, "if a man has a mind to *prance*, he must study at Christ Church…"

Among those who have pranced here down the generations have been Rowan Williams the Archbishop of Canterbury, John Locke the philosopher, El Hassan bin Talal the Crown Prince of Jordan, Edward VII the King of England, Apsley Cherry-Garrard the explorer, Joseph Banks the botanist, William Gladstone the Prime Minister, William Penn the founder of Pennslyvania, John Wesley the founder of Methodism, John Taverner and Howard Goodall the composers, Albert Einstein the scientist, Philip Sidney and W.H. Auden the poets, Richard Hakluyt the geographer, John Ruskin the critic, Lord Shaftesbury the politician who ended underground child employment in England, and Lewis Carroll the mathematician who sent Alice into Wonderland.

Enriched for so long by so many singular minds, with such a range of experience, such variety of character and achievement, it is no wonder that by now Christ Church has achieved the status of an Idea. Redolent with pride and self-amusement, it is often envied, sometimes mocked or even reviled, but it is close to the hearts of nearly all those who have been its members. They call it familiarly The House, from its Latin title – *Aedes Christi*, the House of Christ: as though irreverently to suggest that if the Almighty himself had been an Oxford man, he would surely have studied at Christ Church.

This guide book invites you to share something of their pride and pleasure, and explore the sensations of a grand idea.

Tom Tower and Tom Quad in the snow. ⟳

An angel depicted in the cathedral's Chapel of Remembrance. ⟳

Library window reflections. ⟳

The fountain and wide water basin which stands at the centre of Tom Quad is named after its statue of Mercury. ⟳

3

Cardinal and King

Nothing about Christ Church, Oxford, is simple, and even its beginnings were complex. It was a gift of the Reformation. Its earliest progenitor was the all-powerful Cardinal Wolsey, who in the splendour of his prime as Papal Legate and Lord Chancellor of England decided in 1523 to found a college at Oxford.

He called it Cardinal College, of course, and he associated it with a former Augustinian priory dedicated to a local saint named Frideswide. Hardly had his men started work on a new building, which was to be suitably grandiose, than at the command of King Henry VIII Wolsey was relieved of all his offices and presently died. His incomplete college passed into the possession of the Crown, and in 1532 Henry re-founded it as King Henry VIII's College. This did not last long either, because very soon the Reformation led to the banning of Roman Catholicism, and in 1546 Henry re-founded the college again with a startling innovation. Now it was to be only partly a college, and partly a Church of England cathedral. This made it unique, in Oxford and everywhere else, and so it remains to this day. Oxford's cathedral incorporates the remains of the original priory and is the college chapel too, and even now it is a solecism to speak of Christ Church College.

All this is, so to speak, very Christ Church. The thing was confusing from the start, but worldly. Its coat of arms is still surmounted by a tasseled Cardinal's hat, but through every successive reign its presiding Visitor has been the reigning monarch of England. Charles I actually made it the seat of his monarchy during the English Civil War.

So a sense of consequence has always been an attribute of the House. Physically it is majestic rather than engaging – Christopher Wren's Tom Tower, which houses the six and one quarter ton bell Great Tom, looks positively designed to be iconic, and the Great Quadrangle below it (Tom Quad in the vernacular) has some of the grandeur of a city square. There is not much quaint or even endearing about the college structures, and a stroll around the gallery of portraits in the Dining Hall advertises in particular the spectacular political power of Christ Church alumni down the generations:

13 British Prime Ministers were educated here, and 11 Viceroys of British India. Unlike many Oxford colleges, Christ Church does not have a castellated gateway of military appearance, but the formidable arch beneath Tom Tower, allowing only a glimpse of the stately quadrangle within, is often enough to deter unsuitable strangers.

And inside the porch of the cathedral-chapel this place's involvement with the great world is commemorated in a terrible roster, the list of those of its sons who were killed in the two 20th-century world wars - 256 men in the first war, 228 in the second. In every conflict in which Britain has been engaged, down to the miseries of Afghanistan, we can sadly assume that House men have been involved.

Cardinal Thomas Wolsey. Portrait by Sampson Strong, c. 1610. ⟳

Artist's impression of the proposed Cardinal College. ⟳

Henry VIII (1491-1547), possibly by Master John; given by the king to Christ Church on its foundation in 1546. ⟳

A cardinal's hat, possibly Thomas Wolsey's, is conserved at Christ Church. ⟳

College and Cathedral

Of course much of the nature of Christ Church, like its influence, has depended upon its intimate relationship with the Anglican Church. The academic Dean of Christ Church is the Dean of the cathedral too. For every Prime Minister and Viceroy the college has nurtured down the centuries, there has certainly been a Bishop or an Archbishop.

The presence within the college of the cathedral vitally influences the meaning of the place. It is one of the smallest cathedrals in England, but by no means the least beautiful, and its memorials vividly illustrate Christ Church's symbiotic stance between the spiritual and the secular – the twin porches of its entrance, on the east side of Tom Quad, are like figurative places of transit, from the arrogant display of the quadrangle into inner recesses of mysticism. It is a building full of allusion and speculation: it is directly descended, after all, from an Augustinian priory, and contains in a side chapel a recon-structed shrine to the resilient Frideswide.

The cathedral brings music to Christ Church. It has its own choir school, and since the days of John Taverner, Wolsey's own master of the music, many of the organists and choirmasters of Christ Church have been eminent musicians. Many of the boy choristers, too, who begin their singing careers at Christ Church when they are eight or nine years old, also grow up to be distinguished music professionals. William Walton the composer was one of them: he was matriculated at the House at the age of 16.

Nowadays men and women of many faiths – and none – are members of the House, but the line of choir-boys crossing Tom Quad in their gowns and Canterbury caps, the canons fluttering in their surplices from their canonical residences, the tolling of the cathedral bells on Sunday mornings, the apertures of mystery that are the entrance to the cathedral and the celestial music that so often emerges from them – all these inescapable symptoms confirm the age-old loyalty.

Joie de vivre

One wintry evening Matthew Arnold's Scholar Gypsy, looking down upon Oxford from the nearby heights, and wrapping his cloak around him,

> *… Turned once to watch, while thick the snow-flakes fall,*
> *The line of festal light in Christ Church hall…*

Poor fellow! He doubtless remembered, from easier times, what excellent food they were eating down there, what rare wines flowed, how the laughter rang in the warmth! The House may sometimes seem austere, and often earnest, but throughout its existence it has known how to enjoy itself.

To this day that same Hall, on a proper occasion, can be a very display of festivity. The lights burn all down the long polished tables, and the gilded embossments in the ceiling flicker in response. From the walls the portraits of a hundred dead worthies look down through the half-light, below them serried ranks of junior members laugh, drink and noisily eat, while at the high table the dons and their distinguished guests, lofty in academic garb and eminence, tuck into evidently sustaining food and decidedly cheering wine!

Just the same celebratory scene, in the very same room, has been enacted *mutatis mutandis* for five centuries. Queen Elizabeth I twice came to stay at the House, and dined at that same high table, and was merrily entertained (those who could not get into the Hall were forbidden, on pain of imprisonment, to make "undecent noyse" outside). In 1566 the whole east side of the great quadrangle was given over to the Queen's retinue, and three nights running she attended a play; in 1592 the Dean preached a sermon for her, too.

That festal line of lights is still an excitement, and dining in Christ Church Hall remains an unforgettable experience. Dancing under the stars at a Commemoration Ball is a particular Christ Church pleasure, too, and Eights Week, when the entire University is boisterously involved in a rowing regatta, uniquely involves the House: the River Thames (or Isis, as they call it at Oxford), flows along the edge of Christ Church Meadow, the college's own parkland, and when the boats are racing the shouts and cheering of the exuberant crowds beside the river reverberate across the Meadow into the cloisters and quiet gardens of academe.

Christ Church from the air, looking south-east. ⟲⟲

Tom Tower from the north-west. ⟲

Christ Church rowers at home on the river. ⟳

Idiosyncrasies and individuality

Christ Church has generally been traditional in style, but liberal in ethos. This has undoubtedly contributed to the character of the college, which is rich in paradox and stubborn peculiarity. For example, at 9.05 pm every evening Great Tom sounds 101 times. Why? Because when the college was founded in 1546 its complement of 100 students had to be within the gates by 9.00 pm. Why does it strike at 9.05 pm, then? Because before the advent of Greenwich Mean Time Oxford time was five minutes behind London time. Why 101, rather than 100? Because in 1663 an extra student was admitted. And why does it all still happen that way? *Because.*

Christ Church Deans and Fellows (here called Students, actually – don't ask why) have themselves often been people of formidable individualism. It was said of Dean Cyril Jackson that in the 1780s he ruled the college "as an absolute monarchy of the most ultra-Oriental character." Henry Aldrich, a 17th-century Dean, was not only a composer of merit and an elegant *bon vivant,* but was actually the architect of Peckwater Quadrangle, while his predecessor John Fell, who commissioned Wren to build Tom Tower, was so severe an autocrat that he is chiefly remembered for the undergraduate ditty

> *I do not love thee, Dr Fell.*
> *The reason why I cannot tell.*
> *But this I know, and know full well:*
> *I do not love thee Dr Fell.*

When his father Samuel, a fervent Royalist and an earlier Dean, was evicted in 1648 by Cromwell's Parliamentary Visitors, his wife flatly refused to budge, and she and her children had to be carried out of the Deanery on planks.

In the 19th century Dean Samuel Smith was famously known as Presence of Mind Smith because when a friend of his had fallen into the river and nearly capsized their boat, he reported that since neither of them could swim "if I had not with great presence of mind hit him on the head with the boathook we would *both* have been drowned". In the 18th century Richard

Corbet, Doctor of Divinity, was well known for singing ballads in pubs around town. And C.L. Dodgson, *aku* Lewis Carroll, who taught here for 40 years, counted among his protégés the Cheshire Cat, the Red Queen, the Mad Hatter and Humpty Dumpty, than whom the House has had no more characteristic alumni.

Individualism has thrived among junior members too, and has taken many forms. Especially in the 18th and 19th centuries this is where the sons of the English patriciate came for their years of higher education, and they all too often spent them in high jinks and riotous living. It used to be said then that the only two books a Christ Church undergraduate needed were the Stud Book and the Racing Calendar, and it was actually Dean Aldrich who had bequeathed them the hedonist ditty:

If on my theme I rightly think,
There are five reasons why men drink,
Good wine, a friend, or being dry,
Or lest we should be, by and by,
Or any other reason why…

Today individualism still proudly thrives at Christ Church, but the idle excess has long gone. The college is socially and ethnically diverse now, with able students from around the world. The admission of women students in 1980, the growth in the number of graduate students, the community of talented junior research fellows at the start of their careers – all make for a profound seriousness of academic purpose, laced with an inherited joie de vivre.

Envoi

Thus individuality and religion, romantic tendencies, humour and style and high memories all contribute to the character of Christ Church. Above all, though, it is a place of learning. It always has been. Even Edward Gibbon the historian, who despised 18th-century Oxford, had to admit that at Christ Church learning had been made "a pleasure, a duty and even a fashion".

It is fundamentally a factory of the intellect. Today 428 undergraduates, about half of them women, 214 graduates and 130 professors, tutors

and other academics work within its gates. The college is not exactly autonomous, because it is of course part of the wider institution that is the University of Oxford, but it is largely self-regulated, at least in attitude, and its buildings perfectly express its purposes. They do not seem to sprawl, and their different ages are easily blended. As a whole they are well-mannered, functional, logical, innately generous buildings, laced with grandeur and surprise, and so properly represent the traditions of this place.

Le Corbusier the architect, who said a house was pre-eminently a living-machine, would have approved of the timeless complex that is *Aedes Christi*. It is a handsome mechanism for learning – and for living humanely, too.

Dean Jackson's imposing statue, by F.L. Chantrey (1820), watches over the entrance to the Hall.

Henry Aldrich, Dean of Christ Church 1689-1711.

America's First Lady, Michelle Obama, addressing London school girls in Christ Church's Great Hall.

Her Majesty Queen Elizabeth II visiting Christ Church, with the Dean and Censors.

Timeline

700

1500

727
Death of
St Frideswide in
Saxon site near
River Thames

c. 1150-1210
Construction of
priory by
Augustinian monks

1289
A shrine to
St Frideswide (ABOVE),
venerated for healing
power, is built for
pilgrims

1523
The powerful
Cardinal Wolsey (ABOVE),
right-hand man of
Henry VIII, decides to
found a new college
at Oxford: Cardinal
College

1524
Closure of St
Frideswide's priory
on the orders of
Cardinal Wolsey; the
following year the
priory becomes the
chapel of Cardinal
College

1529
Downfall of Cardinal
Wolsey after his failure
to obtain a divorce
from Catherine of
Aragon for Henry VIII;
the college is
unfinished, with
today's Tom Quad
missing one side

1532
Founding of King
Henry VIII's College
on Wolsey's site

1546
Henry VIII (ABOVE)
refounds the
institution as Christ
Church, combining
college and cathedral
under a dual bequest

1600

1700

1800

1900

2000

1642-46
King Charles I (ABOVE) uses the college as the headquarters of his Parliament during the Civil War

1660-86
The Restoration of the Monarchy and rewards for Christ Church's royalist loyalty usher in a period of construction, masterminded by Dean John Fell; Tom Quad is finally completed

1682
Construction of Tom Tower, designed by Sir Christopher Wren

1713
The Palladian Peckwater Quad is finished, based on designs by Dean Henry Aldrich

1717-72
The Library (ABOVE) is built, also inspired by Dean Aldrich

1856
Arrival of Dean Henry Liddell (ABOVE) and his young family, including Alice

1862-65
Construction of Meadow Buildings

1865
Publication of Lewis Carroll's *Alice's Adventures in Wonderland*

1867
An Act of Parliament replaces the original constitution of 1546

1968
Completion of Blue Boar Quadrangle (ABOVE) and opening of the Picture Gallery

1980
Women are admitted as members of college

2002
Reconstruction of St Frideswide's Shrine

2006
Oxford Literary Festival (ABOVE) first held at Christ Church

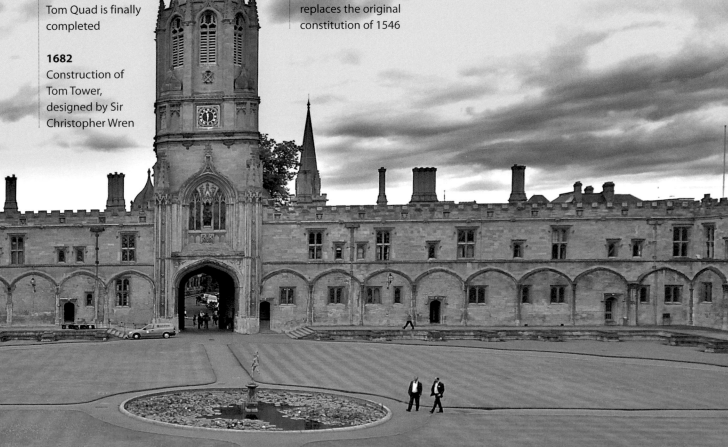

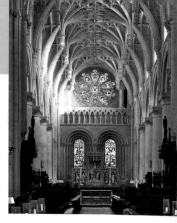

2 The Tour

Peckwater Quad
The pure Palladian architecture of Peckwater Quadrangle has graced Christ Church since 1713. Built to house gentlemen and noblemen, today it provides some of the most beautiful student accommodation in Oxford, allocated by ballot.

Christ Church offers the visitor a unique insight into an institution that has often been at the centre of English history. Founded by an ambitious but ill-fated cardinal, re-founded by a king, and home during the Civil War to yet another king, the college has produced many prime ministers and countless other luminaries in its five centuries of existence.

The fabric of the place – its buildings, gardens and quadrangles – brings this rich history to life, recalling the powerful and sometimes pious individuals who wished to leave their imprint on the college. It also takes us through 500 years – and more when we consider the cathedral's medieval origins – of architectural history, reflecting different styles and tastes from the Tudor period to the present day. Christ Church is history in stone, a living memorial to the past as well as a vibrant modern community.

Not all areas of the college are accessible to visitors, but a tour will take you through the medieval heart of Christ Church – the cloister and parts of the cathedral – as well as the grandiose Tudor-era Tom Quad and the elegant 18th-century Palladian Peckwater Quad. It reveals traces of St Frideswide, the mysterious saint in whose memory the priory, which became the cathedral, was founded. It takes the visitor into the imposing Hall, where generations of students have eaten under the gaze of monarchs and prime ministers, commemorated in portraits. It allows you to linger in the monastic cloister or the vast expanse of Tom Quad, dominated by the unmistakable form of Tom Tower with its great bell.

Before starting the tour, through the imposing Victorian Meadow Building, do not miss the surprisingly rural atmosphere of Christ Church Meadow, where a tree-shaded path leads to the River Thames (or Isis). From Meadow Gate, clearly marked directions then point the way to the cloister, the Hall, Tom Quad and the cathedral before taking the visitor into Peckwater Quad and Canterbury Quad, where the picture gallery – the only one of its kind in Oxford – displays an impressive collection of Old Masters.

Along the way you will notice remarkable architectural features: the fan-vaulted ceiling of the Hall stairs, the intricate ornamentation within the Hall, the graceful symmetry of Peckwater's three matching buildings. You will also catch sight of details that remind us of individuals connected to Christ Church's history: a portrait of Henry VIII, a piece of graffiti directed at Robert Peel, the shrine of a saint. All this reminds us that these buildings, both college and cathedral, have witnessed a long and varied history.

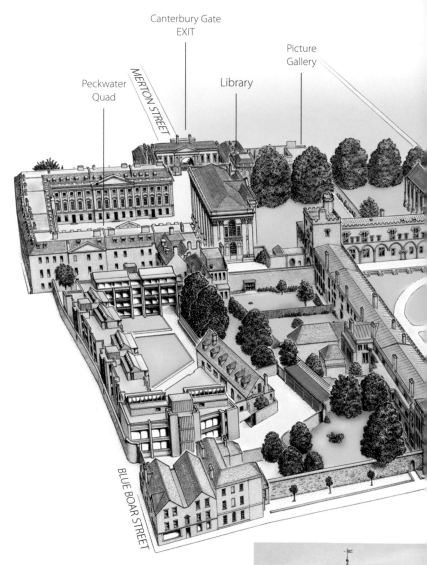

Christ Church Cathedral – *The cathedral was once the monastery church of St Frideswide's Priory, and features a beautiful 15th-century vaulted ceiling.*

The Great Hall
Thomas Wolsey's great dining hall is still the place where college members eat every day.

Meadow Building
The Gothic windows and balconies of Victorian Meadow Building look out across the Christ Church Meadow to the river Isis (or Thames).

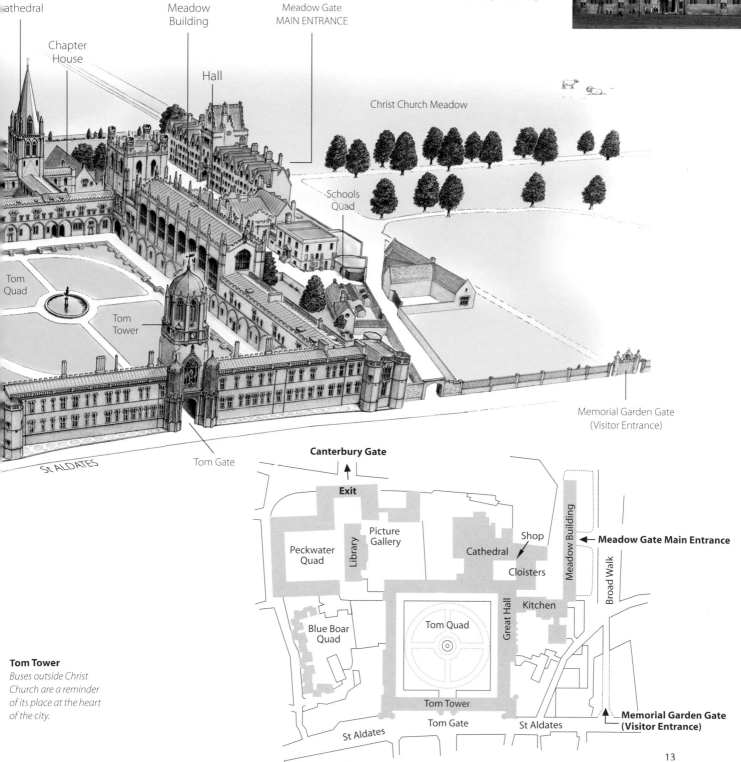

Cathedral

Chapter House

Meadow Building

Hall

Meadow Gate MAIN ENTRANCE

Christ Church Meadow

Schools Quad

Tom Quad

Tom Tower

Memorial Garden Gate (Visitor Entrance)

ST ALDATES

Tom Gate

Tom Tower
Buses outside Christ Church are a reminder of its place at the heart of the city.

Canterbury Gate

Exit

Peckwater Quad

Library

Picture Gallery

Shop

Cathedral

Cloisters

Meadow Building

◄ Meadow Gate Main Entrance

Broad Walk

Blue Boar Quad

Tom Quad

Great Hall

Kitchen

Tom Tower

Tom Gate

St Aldates

St Aldates

Memorial Garden Gate (Visitor Entrance)

The Meadow

The tour of Christ Church starts through the Memorial Garden entrance on St Aldates. Walk through the lavender-lined Memorial Garden and pass the apt inscription from John Bunyan's Pilgrim's Progress until the imposing Meadow Building appears on the left. Stretching ahead and to the right are paths leading through the extensive and beautiful stretch of rural tranquillity known as Christ Church Meadow.

Covering 46 acres, the Meadow includes rich pasture and tree-lined paths and is certainly worth exploring before you enter the college itself. A flood-meadow, bounded by Oxford's two rivers, the Thames and the Cherwell, the area has remained more or less unchanged since medieval times. In 1354, Lady Elizabeth Montacute endowed what was then St Frideswide's priory with half of the present-day Meadow and the land has been held in trust by Christ Church since its foundation. The Meadow was briefly threatened in 1965 when Oxford planners proposed a link road to run through it, but vigorous opposition fortunately defeated the plan.

Turn directly ahead in front of Meadow Building and follow the Poplar Walk, whose trees were planted in 1872 by Dean Liddell, Alice's father. This broad path runs straight down to the Thames (or Isis as it is known in Oxford). During much of the year you will see, on your left, the college's own herd of Longhorn and Aberdeen Angus cattle, grazing on the lush grass. As you reach the river bank turn left and continue straight on until you cross a hump-backed bridge, which leads to a row of college boathouses. Christ Church's, a red brick building adorned with the college's distinctive Wolsey-inspired crest, is the last of these, standing at the confluence of the Thames and Cherwell.

A circular walk with wonderful views of the Oxford skyline skirts the Cherwell and takes you close to the Botanic Garden. Return to the college along the Broad Walk or via Deadman's Walk, named after the route outside the city walls taken by Jewish funeral processions when Oxford's Jews were buried on a site which is now in the Botanic Garden.

The entrance to the college is through the Meadow Building, dating from 1863. Its Venetian style was reputedly favoured by the great art historian and friend of Lewis Carroll, John Ruskin. Ruskin was an undergraduate at the college between 1837 and 1842 and may well have seen the flooded Meadow resembling a watery Venetian landscape.

Visitors, students and local residents stroll through the Meadow while punters enjoy the tranquil pleasures of the river. ⮕

Pheasants and deer, herons and kingfishers, geese and ducks are all at home here. ⬇

The path through Christ Church Meadow. ⬆

A footbridge leads from college boathouses lining the Isis. ⮕

The crest greets visitors as they enter the Memorial Gardens from St Aldates. ⮕

A plaque on the wall of the Meadow's 'Dead Man's Walk' commemorates the 1784 balloon flight of James Sadler. ⮕

Meadow Building and its Gothic tower were finished in 1865 to accommodate increasing numbers of undergraduates. ⮕

Christ Church's visitor entrance, Meadow Gate. ⮌

Meadow Building and the cathedral spire rise beyond the Meadow, where Christ Church's Longhorn cattle graze. ⮕

James Sadler
1753 – 1828

First English Aeronaut
who in a fire balloon
made a successful
ascent from near this
place 4th October 1784
to land near Woodeaton

The spectacular ceiling above the stairs to the Hall was created in the 19th century and above it hang the cathedral's twelve bells. ⬆

Former students return as 'old members' in gowns or doctoral robes to dine at Gaudy dinners. ➷

The cathedral cloister dates to the 12th century and connects the cathedral and monastery buildings. ➷➷

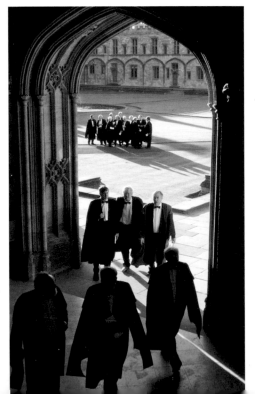

The Cloister and Hall Stairs

The cloister, like the cathedral to which it leads, is part of St Frideswide's priory, the ancient church from which the modern-day cathedral is descended. Human remains from the 8th-century era of St Frideswide have been discovered in the central plot, but part of the cloister itself dates from the 12th and 13th centuries and the rest from the 15th and 19th centuries. There were once four sides, but the west walk was removed by Cardinal Wolsey to form stairs leading to the Hall.

The cloister is Gothic in style, built from attractive golden stone, and features a rib-vaulted ceiling similar to that found in the cathedral itself. Its walls display coats of arms, memorials and figurative carvings, and on one section of restored stone vaulting are the faces of Queen Victoria and Lord Salisbury, the monarch and prime minister of the day. An olive tree, symbolising healing and reconciliation, and a modern fountain decorate the inner space of the cloister and remind us of the cathedral's spiritual purpose.

The spacious and beautiful Chapter House currently contains the cathedral's gift shop and dates from about 1225, but the door leading into it from the cloister is even earlier and is Norman with characteristic zigzag moulding. The Chapter House was originally where the Augustinian monks who founded the priory would have met, and in succeeding centuries it has served as a dining room and lecture theatre. Now visitors can admire its rich carvings and intricate vaulting, including grotesque imps and a touching roof carving of the Virgin and Child. Mural paintings of St Peter and St Paul, bearing keys and sword respectively, adorn the vaulted ceiling.

Along with an array of stained glass, the Chapter House also displays some of Christ Church's valuable gold and silver artefacts as well as items loaned by parishes within the Diocese of Oxford.

Steps lead from the cloister up to the tower and to a wide stone staircase. This imposing approach to the Hall, with the spectacular 1640 fan-vaulted ceiling above, is one of the college's most recognised locations, the setting for scenes in the first two Harry Potter films. Below a wooden door carries the mysterious message 'No Peel', reputedly made with hot pokers. The message was directed at Sir Robert Peel, a former Christ Church undergraduate, who as Home Secretary controversially supported the 1829 Catholic Emancipation Act. It may well be among the earliest surviving examples of student graffiti.

The fountain and olive tree in the cloisters provide a tranquil place to rest at times, or a busy point from which to grasp the layout of the medieval monastery. ⇨

College crest in the Hall vaulting. ⇨⇨

The famous 'No Peel' door at the foot of the Hall stairs. ⇨⇨

The Hall: architecture

If the cathedral and cloister recall the legacy of St Frideswide, the Hall is testimony to the grand designs of Cardinal Wolsey. Alas, he barely lived to see the great room that he planned for feasts in his new college, as it was finished in 1529, the year of his disgrace. From 1525 Wolsey poured a fortune into the building of the Hall and its

Kitchen, employing the best craftsmen of the age. It was finished by the time of his death and has remained largely as he ordered it. Only the windows have been altered, and the roof after a fire in 1720.

The largest pre-Victorian college hall in Oxford or Cambridge, it measures 115 by 40 feet and is 50 feet high. One of its most distinctive features is the imposing wooden 'hammerbeam' ceiling, which avoids the need for pillars or posts for support. This was the work of the royal carpenter Humphrey Coke, and the absence of pillars adds to the sense of space. Light is provided through 17 windows, most placed high above wooden panelled walls. These panels insulated the otherwise chilly Hall, which was heated by open wood fires.

Most of the Hall's windows originally carried extensive heraldic designs but these were largely replaced with plain glass in the 18th century. Two important heraldic decorations remain, however. Cardinal Wolsey's arms are depicted beneath a red cardinal's hat on the roof posts, while Henry VIII's arms predictably take the central positions on the walls. Over 600 badges, devices and coats of arms adorn the ceiling.

The Hall is nowadays used mostly for meals, but during the Civil War King Charles I, who had made the college his headquarters, held meetings of his Parliament (as distinct from the opposing Westminster Parliament) in this room from 1643 to 1645. In May 1645 a 'bullet of IX lb. weight' was fired by Parliamentarians in distant Marston and struck the north side of the Hall.

There are several reminders of *Alice's Adventures in Wonderland*, including the window (the fifth on the left from the entrance) showing portraits of Alice, Lewis Carroll and some of the book's creatures. The brass firedogs guarding the fireplace opposite bear an uncanny resemblance to Alice when in the story her neck grows unnaturally long. More recently, the Hall was the inspiration for various scenes in the Harry Potter films, but the studio replica was wider with room for four rows of tables.

Alice in Wonderland firedogs in the Great Hall.

Wolsey's Great Hall on Tom Quad's southern side.

The Hall is a spectacular setting, whether for a fine dinner ↷ or a hasty student brunch. ↻

The Hall: function

The Hall is in almost constant use and is in many ways the heart of the college's daily life. It has been estimated that no fewer than 200,000 meals are served each year to Christ Church's academic community and those attending conferences and other events.

Breakfast and lunch are served to college members on a self-service basis, but dinner is normally a more elaborate affair. There are usually two sittings, Informal Hall at 6.20 pm and Formal Hall at 7.20 pm. At Formal Hall undergraduates are expected to wear gowns, while senior members dine at High Table at the west end of the Hall.

The dramatic approach up the magnificent staircase and the sheer size of the Hall make dining here a memorable occasion, even when experienced on a daily basis. The architecture, portraits and atmosphere link present-day members to a tradition that stretches back almost five hundred years.

The High Table, around which sit up to 30 senior members and their guests, is elevated on a dais or platform, as far away as possible from any draughts from the open door. Those at High Table enter the Hall from the Senior Common

Room up a spiral staircase and pass through a door on the south side. On special occasions college silver decorates the High Table.

Before dinner commences a Latin grace is read by an undergraduate scholar. Most dinners consist of three courses, and undergraduates are free to sit at the long lamp-lit tables with their friends. One table is normally reserved for graduate students. Wine, beer and other drinks can be bought from the adjacent Buttery.

The Hall also often hosts special dinners – guest nights, meals organised by clubs and societies, feasts to celebrate sporting triumphs.

Although the Hall caters principally for the academic community, it is also the centrepiece of the many courses, summer schools and other special activities that take place in Christ Church. Old members or alumni are also regularly invited back to college and dine with their contemporaries in the Hall's spectacular setting at a reunion dinner called a Gaudy.

Wooden panelling is the backdrop to portraits of former Deans and royal 'Visitors' as well as other important old members. ➔

Henry VIII, attributed to John Taylor, 17th century, after Holbein ; John Locke, after Sir Godfrey Kneller (1646-1723); Sir Dudley Carleton, Anonymous. ↻

Elizabeth I, Anonymous; Charles Dodgson (Lewis Carroll), Sir Hubert von Herkomer (1849-1915); W.H. Auden, Robert Buhler (1969-1989); John Wesley, George Romney (1734-1802). ➔

The Hall: portraits

Generations of Christ Church undergraduates have dined in Hall under the gaze of many famous and influential people associated with the college. On all of its four sides this great room is lined with portraits, spanning the centuries between the college's foundation and the present day.

Above the High Table are portraits of a number of past Deans. A tiny-waisted and fiery-headed Elizabeth I is also present next to her father Henry VIII, who displays the bulky physique of his later years. To his left is Cardinal Wolsey who appears – rather rashly, given his eventual downfall – to be wagging a stern finger at the king. In this pictorial arrangement the founder of Cardinal College and his nemesis, the founder of Christ Church, are again close to one another. Below is a bust of Queen Elizabeth II, Visitor of Christ Church, by the Croatian-born sculptor Oscar Nemon.

Other portraits recall the college's role in producing men of original and radical intellect. John Locke (1632-1704) was a highly influential Enlightenment figure whose liberal thinking inspired the American Declaration of Independence. John Wesley (1703-91) was an undergraduate and ordained here in 1727 before going on to lead the movement that became Methodism. Another non-conformist was William Penn (1644-1718) who later became a Quaker and founded Pennsylvania. Edward Pusey (1800-82), Regius Professor of Hebrew and a canon at Christ Church, was a founding member of the controversial Oxford Movement, which sought to reconcile the Anglican Church with Roman Catholicism. Pusey was a friend of Charles Dodgson, the alias of 'Lewis Carroll'.

Lewis Carroll is, of course, present among the portraits in a picture that captures his shy and sensitive nature. It was painted after his death from photographs. A more modern portrait captures the distinctive features of W. H. Auden (1907-73), one of the major poets of the 20th century. Auden read English at Christ Church, revisited during his years as Oxford's Professor of Poetry and in his last declining months accepted the offer of a cottage in the college's grounds.

Last but not least come six of the thirteen British prime ministers educated here. Perhaps most imposing is William Ewart Gladstone (1809-1898) who held the office four times. His stern expression was perfectly captured by the eminent Pre-Raphaelite painter John Everett Millais, who married John Ruskin's wife after she and Ruskin parted.

24

St Frideswide and the medieval legacy

The cathedral's origins predate those of the college by around 800 years and are to be found in the 8th-century legend of St Frideswide, patron saint of Oxford. Born the daughter of Didan, King of Oxford, Frideswide chose a devout and monastic life but was pursued by King Algar, who wished to marry her. This legend tells of him being struck blind by divine intervention and Frideswide fled into the countryside, later finding her religious sanctuary in a monastery close to the River Thames. This early Saxon site, about which we know little, marks the beginning of the present-day cathedral and it was here that she was buried in 727. A monastery church or priory was subsequently built by Augustinian monks from around 1150 to 1210 and named after St Frideswide. The central part of today's building dates from that era.

Entering by the West Door, keep to the left via the North Transept to reach the Latin Chapel, the part of the cathedral most associated with St Frideswide, and its medieval heart. Here is her shrine, built in 1289 when the saint had become an object of veneration and pilgrimage due to her healing miracles. This, the cathedral's oldest monument, once contained her relics but was destroyed during the religious turmoil of the Reformation. Painstaking restoration work, with parts of the original structure found within Christ Church and put together again, allowed the shrine to be placed close to where it is thought that she is buried. The shrine, like other decorations in the cathedral, carries details of plants and leaves – perhaps a reference to her escape into the woods. Fittingly, it stands under the colourful 1859 stained glass depiction of her life by Edward Burne-Jones. A nearby 14th-century window shows Frideswide or Frideswida bearing a crown.

The shrine is overlooked by the Watching Loft, an elaborately carved wooden gallery on top of a stone plinth. It is believed that during the heyday of the St Frideswide pilgrimage cult a monk would watch over the shrine from this vantage point to ensure that nobody stole the money or gifts left by pilgrims.

Also close to the shrine is the tomb of Lady Elizabeth Montecute, who died in 1354. She was a generous benefactor to St Frideswide's priory, leaving half of the land that makes up the Meadow. Images of her ten children surround the base of her tomb, which was moved from the next-door Lady Chapel bringing her close – as she had asked – to the saint's relics.

The tomb of Lady Elizabeth Montecute. ↷↷

The Virgin Mary depicted in 14th-century glass in the Latin Chapel. ↷

The cathedral Chancel's magnificent vaulted ceiling. ↴

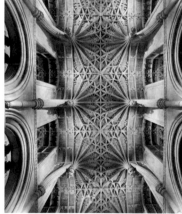

Robert King, the first Bishop of Oxford, commemorated in a window in the Chapel of Remembrance made by Bernard van Linge. ↷

The shrine of St Frideswide stands in the Latin Chapel of the cathedral and is overlooked by the Burne-Jones window, which tells her story, and the medieval Watching Loft. ↷↷

From Priory to Cathedral

Thomas Wolsey and Thomas More, commemorated in windows in the Great Hall. ↻

The ceiling of the medieval refectory pulpit in what is now Old Library still bears its original red and blue paintwork, and golden stars, giving a sense of the original paint scheme of the Priory chapel. ↻

The cathedral is a wonderful venue for musical events and concerts as well as worship. ↻

Passing through the Lady Chapel into the North Choir Aisle, we see the Bell Altar. The cathedral's most modern feature, it contrasts with Frideswide's ancient shrine and commemorates former Christ Church man and Bishop of Chichester, George Bell, who courageously condemned the Allied bombing of German cities during the Second World War.

Moving into the Chancel, we can now view evidence of the various stages of the cathedral's development. The monastery church or priory of St Frideswide continued until 1524, when it was closed by Cardinal Wolsey. Towards the end of its monastic period it was adorned with the spectacular ceiling above the Chancel. Employing the late medieval style of rib vaulting, William Orchard constructed an intricate system of twelve lantern-shaped pendants that appear to hang in the air, while small ribs and stone meet together at the vault's centre to form eight pointed symbolic stars – representing heaven.

The High Altar is Victorian, and next to it stands the Bishop's Throne or *kathedra* in Greek, from which all cathedrals take their name – the present throne dates from 1955. The Bishop of Oxford occupies this seat during ordinations and special services such as at Christmas and Easter. Above it are the Arms of the Diocese of Oxford, featuring the emblematic ox fording the Thames.

The Bishop's Throne reminds us of the building's unique dual function as cathedral and college chapel, and a nearby window image of the first Bishop of Oxford, Robert King, recalls the transformation of St Frideswide's priory into the cathedral. In 1525 the church became the college chapel of Wolsey's Cardinal College. Then, in 1546, after Henry VIII became the Head of the Church of England and created several new bishoprics and dioceses (among them Oxford), the chapel was turned as well into a cathedral.

There had previously been a short-lived Oxford Cathedral (1542-46) at Osney, to the west of the city. This former abbey was abandoned and demolished, and most of its property, including the Great Tom bell, was transferred to the newly named Christ Church. The stained glass representation of Bishop King, from around 1630, shows the already ruined Osney Abbey and the tower that used to house Great Tom.

To the right of the Chancel (if facing the High Altar) is the cathedral's oldest window (*c.* 1320) in the Lucy Chapel, depicting the martyrdom of St Thomas Becket. The original saint's face was removed during the Reformation to prevent the destruction of the window.

The Cathedral today

Christ Church's unique history, with its dual foundation, means that the cathedral is unlike any other in the Church of England. In some respects it performs the functions of a normal cathedral, acting as the mother church of the Diocese of Oxford, the fifth largest in England with 625 parishes and 813 churches. But it is different for one important reason – it is also a college chapel. This double role has created an institution in which the academic and the religious are closely intertwined. The Dean, the

equivalent in other Oxford colleges to the Master or Principal, must be an ordained priest, while the ecclesiastical foundation has also bequeathed to the college a number of Canon Professors. Christ Church is still the patron of eighty parishes across the country, from Cornwall to North Lancashire, as a result of historic land holdings.

Nowadays the cathedral is a busy and vibrant place of worship, with at least three services on almost every day of the year and six on Sundays during term time.

The Choir

One of the cathedral's greatest assets is its choir, an institution that dates back to Cardinal Wolsey five centuries ago. The tradition of sacred music has lasted up to the present day, and the choir is now not only heard in the cathedral's daily services but on international tours, radio, TV, film, and numerous audio recordings.

The musical foundation consists of an organist, sub-organist, two organ scholars, and a choir of 12 men and 16 boys. Six of the men are undergraduates – Academical Clerks – the others are professional singers. The boys attend Christ Church Cathedral School, across St Aldates in Brewer Street, which offers small classes from nursery up to the age of 13. Not all the children who attend the school are cathedral choristers, but some are selected for their musical ability and offered scholarships, and some sing in the choir at Worcester College, Oxford. In total, about 160 children attend the school.

The choir has enjoyed a strong media profile in recent years, and several of its recordings have won international awards. The choir has appeared on the award-winning TV series *Big Bangs*, presented by Howard Goodall, a Christ Church graduate in Music, as well as singing his themes to the popular *Mr Bean* and *The Vicar of Dibley* TV series, written by Christ Church English graduate Richard Curtis. Other famous alumni from Christ Church include the eminent 20th-century composer Sir William Walton, who was a chorister, and Sir Adrian Boult.

The Cathedral Choir leading worship on Palm Sunday. ⌃

The Cloister fountain provides inspiration for all ages. ⌄

Boys of the choir can relax sometimes too. ⌃

The Eucharist or Holy Communion is celebrated daily in the cathedral. ⌄

29

Tom Quad

Pass through the Cloister once more and a sign directs you to Tom Quad. This enormous quadrangle, the largest in Oxford, measures 264 by 261 feet. Originally known as the Great Quadrangle, it was renamed in the 17th century when the great six-ton Tom Bell was installed in the tower that Sir Christopher Wren designed to sit on top of the gatehouse. There is more on Tom Bell and Tom Tower on page 56.

We have seen that Cardinal Wolsey had ambitious plans for the quadrangle, including perhaps the demolition of the chapel and the construction of a vast replacement on the north side. In the event, this never happened and Wolsey fell together with his grand vision. He lived to see three sides finished but the north side remained uncompleted for more than a century, little more than a low wall. Nor did his scheme to have the entire quadrangle adorned by cloisters

Drama and spectacle illuminate Tom Quad at the Christ Church Commemoration Ball.

come to fruition. The arches that stretch around the quadrangle's wall mark where these cloisters might have protruded out to the edge of the raised walkway. This may help to explain the spaciousness of Tom Quad and what some see as its austerity.

In the 1630s and 1640s work finally began on completing the quadrangle. For too long it had been an eyesore, with a muddy track used by townsfolk and cattle. The autocratic Dean John Fell (1625-86) determinedly collected money and pushed through a building plan that at last unified the four sides into a harmonious whole. He also oversaw the excavation of the soil that created the grassed recess (the earth was used to make the Broad Walk in the Meadow) and installed the circular basin in its middle. But perhaps his greatest legacy to the college was his decision to commission Sir Christopher Wren to

finish Wolsey's gatehouse. Within a year, in 1682, the gigantic domed tower was in place, dominating both the quadrangle and the south of the city.

Dean Fell utterly changed the look of Tom Quad and is commemorated by a statue in the tower named after him in its north-eastern corner. It has been pointed out, however, that it bears little resemblance to Dean Fell, who was 'a thin grave man'.

Tom Quad has been renovated in succeeding centuries but remains much as the forceful Dean left it. The statue in the central pond has been replaced twice, once after a student prank in 1817, and is now a replica of the statue of Mercury in Florence, by Giambologna (1529-1608).

A music student prepares an essay in a panelled room in Peckwater Quad. ⟳

Peckwater Quad. ⟳

Peckwater Quad

Through the archway in the north-east corner of Tom Quad lies the college's second biggest quadrangle, Peckwater Quad (known simply as 'Peck' to undergraduates). It stands on the site of the medieval Peckwater Inn which was donated to St Frideswide's priory in 1246. It is quite different in style and extent from Tom Quad and is an exceptional example of classical symmetry.

This quadrangle was the work of another exceptional Dean, in this case Henry Aldrich (1649-1710) who was something of a polymath: scholar, churchman, musician, collector and architect. Aware that the college needed to replace the old Peckwater Inn, which had been turned into quadrangular accommodation not long before, Dean Aldrich sought funding and in 1705 received a generous gift of £2,000 from Anthony Radcliffe, a Canon of Christ Church and the donor of the first Mercury statue. His name is inscribed with suitable prominence on the central frieze.

The old buildings were soon swept away and work began on the new quadrangle, overseen by master-mason William Townesend. By 1713 the three sides that we see now were completed, but Dean Aldrich had already died three years earlier, unable to see his great project take final shape. It was considered a masterpiece of Palladian architecture, echoing the harmony and uniformity popularised in the 17th and 18th centuries by the Venetian architect Andrea Palladio. The great architectural historian Nikolaus Pevsner describes it as 'impeccably uniform'.

Each of the three sides – the fourth is occupied by the library – has fifteen bays and

each is two and a half storeys high decorated with Ionic pilasters. The centre of each range also has a five-bay section with six great pillars and a pediment. Inside the building the emphasis is also on symmetry with each set of rooms comprising a large front room and two smaller back rooms. Not surprisingly, these 'sets' were much sought after, especially as increasing numbers of wealthy, aristocratic young men were coming to Christ Church during this time. Nowadays the sitting room will be shared by a two undergraduates with a small bedroom each.

Peckwater Quad was the scene of a small riot in 1927, when members of the elitist Bullingdon Club, a university dining club, reportedly smashed 468 windows and several doors after an extended drinking spree. The club was subsequently banned from meeting in Oxford. The quadrangle was refaced in 1931 and has happily never experienced another such event.

Dean Henry Aldrich's original design for the new Quad. Building work commenced in 1706.

Undergraduates and graduates study in the lower library. ⬆➡

Christ Church Library. ⬇

The Library

The south side of Peckwater Quad comprises the library, begun in 1717 but not finished until 1772. This was also the brainchild of Dean Aldrich, who submitted a plan in 1705 for a building based on the Palace of Versailles and so probably intended it for residential use. He died before work could begin, but his donation to the college of a large collection of books and manuscripts hastened the construction of a new library to replace the original, which dated from 1562 and was situated in the cloister. This first library, in a former priory refectory, had run out of space by the end of the 17th century.

Some of Dean Aldrich's design was kept, but Canon Stratford remarked ambitiously in 1716 that the college should create 'the finest library that belongs to any society in Europe'. An architect, George Clarke, was hired, but progress was slow as donations trickled in and building work was often postponed. The original plan envisaged a first-floor library with an open loggia on the ground floor, but this layout was abandoned in the 1760s due to another bequest – this time by General John Guise (1682-1765), who left Christ Church his valuable

collection of two thousand drawings and two hundred paintings. It was suddenly necessary to find a home for this collection, and the ground floor was converted into two separate rooms. Further bequests rapidly filled the library with books, pamphlets and even coins and scientific instruments as well as the works of art.

When finished the library presented a more Baroque face than the rest of Peckwater Quad, with seven broad bays separated by giant Corinthian columns. Inside – and visitors are not permitted to enter as it is primarily a place of study – is an elegant staircase with a wrought-iron handrail leading past a statue of John Locke.

There is a bust of Dean Aldrich and a bronze of the 20th-century Dean John Lowe by Jacob Epstein.

The ground floor consists of the two reading rooms, separated by the entrance hall. Nowadays there is access to computers and a busy book loaning system. The East Room contains a Victorian-era gallery added to hold the ever-growing collection of books, while the West Room was until 1968 the home for many of Guise's paintings. These were finally removed in 1968 to the brand-new purpose-built Picture Gallery. A few portraits of clergymen still adorn this peaceful room, used by generations of students.

The Picture Gallery

Christ Church is the only college in either Oxford or Cambridge to possess a collection of Old Masters large enough to merit a picture gallery. This is in a large part due to the generosity of General John Guise (1682-1765), who – as we have seen – left the college almost two thousand drawings and over two hundred paintings, which were kept in the Library until the 1960s. Many of the artworks and objects that were donated to the college and temporarily housed in the Library were subsequently re-distributed to other institutions and galleries, but the paintings, drawings and prints were kept by Christ Church as an important collection in their own right.

Guise's donation had been preceded by a large gift of prints from Dean Henry Aldrich, himself the inspiration behind what was to become the Library. Guise was an undergraduate while Aldrich was Dean and was treated as a nobleman by Aldrich and allowed to dine at High Table. In later life the military man became a prominent collector, described by Horace Walpole as 'a very brave officer … and a great connoisseur of pictures'. His collection was mostly of Italian works, including drawings by Leonardo, Bellini, Raphael and Michelangelo but also lesser-known artists from the 16th and 17th centuries. He also acquired work from Spain, Flanders and the Netherlands.

Later pioneer collectors gave the college valuable gifts. William Thomas Horner Fox-Strangways (1795-1865) presented 38 early Italian paintings, including Filippo Lippi's *The Wounded Centaur*, and Walter Savage Landor (1775-1864), the eminent Victorian poet, was particularly interested in religious 'primitives'.

The college's burgeoning collection was eventually too much for the Library to hold, and while some paintings were distributed around the college, it was nevertheless decided to create a purpose-built picture gallery as a permanent home. This allowed the paintings to be properly conserved in an appropriate environment.

The Picture Gallery, designed by Powell & Moya, was opened in 1968 and soon won widespread approval for its innovative modernist features in highly traditional surroundings. Largely subterranean, it is accessed in the small Canterbury Quad but stretches into the Deanery garden, allowing natural light into its various gallery spaces. Most of the Old Masters are on permanent display, but drawings are selected and regularly changed as a conservation precaution. A small entrance fee allows visitors to admire one of the most important collections of Renaissance Baroque and early Italian art in the United Kingdom.

The innovative modernist Powell & Moya building that houses the Picture Gallery allows much natural light to illuminate the galleries and blends in well with the traditional architecture of the college. It was opened by HM The Queen in 1968. ☉

'A Boy Drinking' by Annibale Carracci (1560-1609). ⏷

'Madonna and Child with Three Angels' by Piero della Francesca (c. 1415-1492). ⏷

The Picture Gallery consists of several exhibition spaces. Most of the space is devoted to the permanent collection, although there is some scope for temporary exhibitions of appropriate quality. Differing sized rooms and corridors allow for larger and smaller pieces to be shown to their best advantage, while a combination of natural and artificial light means that they are appropriately lit at all times of day. The large central Main Gallery is where the Baroque Old Masters are on show. The smaller drawings and prints are kept in display cases.

Among the extensive collection of drawings is Leonardo da Vinci's *A Grotesque Head*, a striking depiction of idealised ugliness that reflects the artist's interest in all aspects of the human form, whether beautiful or not. The drawings by Michelangelo include a remarkable anatomical study, a red chalk drawing of a tautly muscled left leg. This is thought to date from the period when Michelangelo was working on the ceiling of the Sistine Chapel in Rome. Other drawings from the Guise Bequest are Giovanni Bellini's enigmatic *Portrait of a Man*, probably dating from around the 1480s, and Andrea del Verrocchio's *Head of a Young Woman*, a fluid and beautiful study by the accomplished draughtsman/sculptor from Florence.

The paintings range from early 14th-century to late 18th-century and are often of religious subjects. An early altarpiece perhaps from Siena shows an enthroned Virgin and Child as well as – unusually for the period – a woman, possibly the patron of the work, kneeling at the foot of the throne. *Madonna and Child with Three Angels*, from the 15th-century artist Piero della Francesca, treats the same theme, but here, in a touchingly natural detail, the Christ Child sucks his fingers with an expression of thoughtful apprehension.

There are also portraits, often commissioned by the rich and powerful of their age. Tintoretto's *Portrait of a Gentleman*, probably from around 1550, shows a self-confident individual, dressed in opulent black silk and fur. Altogether more unusual, however, is the large canvas that used to hang among the smoke and steam of the Kitchen. Annibale Carracci's *The Butcher's Shop*, painted in the 1580s, offers a remarkably naturalistic portrait of a group of butchers at work, with carcasses, cuts of meat and even a live sheep painted in vivid detail. The novelty of the subject matter depicted and its monumental size allow many interpretations of *The Butcher's Shop*. One hypothesis is that it was a family portrait, another that it was a shop-sign and yet another interprets the boldness in topic and vivacity of the brush stroke as a painting about painting.

'The Butcher's Shop' by
Annibale Carracci (1560-
1609). ⬆

'Head of a Young Woman'
by Andrea del Verrocchio
(1435-88). ↻

'Soldier on Horseback' by
Sir Anthony van Dyck
(1599-1641). ↻↻

Life at Christ Church

3

The academic community

Christ Church's unique dual foundation as cathedral and college means that its academic structure is different from that of other Oxford colleges. Its Dean is always an ordained Anglican appointed by the Crown, while six resident Canons include academics specialising in theological subjects. In all there are about 65 members of the Governing Body of whom the great majority are officially known as Students. In fact, they are what in other colleges would be called Fellows and most of them are also Tutors. They are appointed not only to teach undergraduates and supervise graduates, but to conduct advanced research in their own fields, and many of them are scholars of international distinction.

A very wide range of subjects is taught in the college, including all the major science and arts disciplines. As elsewhere in Oxford, undergraduates are usually expected to attend lectures or practical science lessons outside the college in their subject-specific faculty but are also taught within the college by their Tutor.

The weekly tutorial is one of the distinctive and most treasured aspects of the University's academic traditions. It involves a face-to-face meeting, often an hour long, between the Tutor and normally one or two students. They are expected to have completed a piece of work, an essay in arts subjects, which is then discussed. Some Tutors

expect undergraduates to read the essay aloud or may read and mark it beforehand. The discussion in a very small group allows Tutors to relate to undergraduates' academic strengths and weaknesses in a way that is not possible in larger seminars. It is essentially a participatory exercise, with undergraduates encouraged to express their views rather than simply being lectured.

In previous centuries Christ Church had a hierarchical system, with aristocratic students ('gentlemen-commoners') given preferential treatment over more humble scholars. Such favouritism is long gone, as is the college's reputation as a haunt for the idle well-to-do. Nowadays all undergraduates must undergo a rigorous entrance procedure, based on exam results and interview, and all are equal on arriving in college. Awards, known as scholarships and exhibitions, are earned through hard work and strong results, normally in the first year. Most undergraduate courses are three years, but some are longer.

A league table of college results in final examinations – the Norrington Table – is published each year, and Christ Church usually appears in the top third. About 15 per cent of students gain first-class degrees, with the largest number attaining an upper second. To keep them on track, undergraduates are expected to sit a mock examination on the Friday before each term starts, called collections.

Undergraduates and graduates study hard and train in a wide range of subjects, but live together as one academic community. ⊖

Student life

Christ Church has the second largest number of students among the Oxford colleges, with approximately 430 undergraduates and 215 postgraduates. Of these about half are women, a proportion that has been growing since women were first admitted into the college in 1980. Students come from a very broad range of educational and social backgrounds; Christ Church has one of the largest access and outreach programmes of any of the Oxford colleges, including open days, teachers' workshops and visits to schools.

Unusually, Christ Church is able to accommodate all its students throughout their courses within college property, although they are free to live outside if they choose to. One advantage of living in college is the steady supply of good and inexpensive food in the Hall.

The academic year is divided into three terms – Michaelmas, Hilary and Trinity – each lasting eight weeks. During a term an undergraduate reading an arts subject can expect up to two tutorials a week, and an essay or another piece of written work is normally expected for each of these. There are also university lectures in all subjects, and those studying languages have intensive teaching in

these. On the science side, there are not only lectures but practical sessions in laboratories. Although the term may be short, the workload is heavy. Most undergraduates use the vacations to read ahead or to revise topics already covered, and each term begins with a mock examination designed to monitor progress.

Final examinations are the culmination of the student's course, and may last a week or two. Most take place in the Examination Schools on the High Street, and students are still required to wear the traditional sub-fusc attire of gowns, dark suits or skirts and white bow ties.

Student life is not entirely about work, however, and Christ Church, like other colleges, has a lively programme of social and sporting events. There are regular discos held in the Junior Common Room as well as occasional fancy dress parties and 'formal' dinners in Hall. Every three years the college holds a much larger Commemoration Ball, which features a range of performers and activities and which takes place at the end of Trinity (summer) Term.

Christ Church has a particularly enviable reputation for rowing, and both men's and women's teams compete in the inter-college competitions that take place in February and May each year – called Torpids and Eights Week. These races finish near the college boathouses that are situated on the riverside part of the Meadow and attract huge crowds of supporters and onlookers. The college is also one of the best at football and rugby, and teams compete in leagues against other colleges.

Christ Church's sportsground is situated beyond the Meadow near the University sportsground at Iffley Road.

Studying chemistry in the Masters' Garden. ↶

Learning the traditional way in Christ Church Library. ↷

Early morning mist for rowing practice on the Isis. ↳

Students relax with sports and many other activities after long hours in laboratories, libraries and lectures. ↳↳

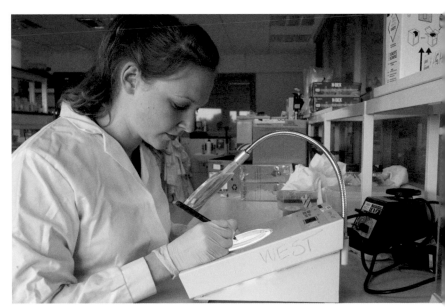

43

Making a mark

Christ Church's list of alumni (former members) is long and distinguished. It includes statesmen, eminent scientists, influential churchmen and world-famous musicians, composers and writers. Some stayed or returned to the college to teach and conduct research, but more went into the wider world to leave their mark in many different fields. Almost all mentioned here are men, but women, admitted since 1980, will doubtless soon form their own list.

William Ewart Gladstone (1809-98), politician, by Sir John Millais (1829-1896). ⊙

John Ruskin (1819-1900), aesthete. ⊘

Howard Goodall (1958-), composer. ⊙

William Penn (1644-1718), Quaker philosopher, copy by Alice Mumford Roberts. ⊙

Politicians and Statesmen

Of the 13 prime ministers who studied at the college, perhaps the most famous is William Gladstone (1809-98), the Liberal leader who in a 60-year career held the office of prime minister four times. He was preceded earlier in the 19th century by the Conservative Sir Robert Peel (1788-1850), who was prime minister twice and was responsible as Home Secretary for the creation of a modern police force, hence the term 'bobbies'. The first Christ Church alumnus to become prime minister was George Grenville (1702-70), whose tax-raising Stamp Act of 1765 strained relations with the North American colonies, while the most recent was Sir Alec Douglas-Home (1903-95), the only prime minister to have played first class cricket.

Scientists and Explorers

The college has always encouraged enquiring minds, and few were more curious than Richard Hakluyt (c.1552-1616), whose writings on travel and navigation were instrumental in the colonisation of North America. William Penn (1644-1718), a Quaker and champion of democracy, was inspired by Hakluyt and went on to found the state of Pennsylvania. Another great traveller was Sir Joseph Banks (1743-1820), who as a botanist and patron of the sciences accompanied Captain Cook on his first three-year trip of exploration. Robert Hooke (1635-1703) was another important scientist, remembered for his role in formulating Hooke's Law while a chorister at Christ Church.

Musicians and Writers

Music has been at the heart of Christ Church since its foundation, and the great composer John Taverner (c.1490-1545) was appointed the first organist and choir master by Cardinal Wolsey in 1526. He has been followed by many distinguished musicians, while composers such as William Walton (1902-83) and more recently Howard Goodall, and the conductor Sir Adrian Boult, have been choristers or undergraduates at the college. Christ Church has also nurtured many writers of repute, not least Sir Philip Sidney (1554-86), the Elizabethan courtier and poet who popularised the sonnet form. The critic and aesthete John Ruskin (1819-1900) was an erratic undergraduate but went on to become a spokesman for the Pre-Raphaelite movement. The scriptwriter Richard Curtis, best known for his film *Four Weddings and a Funeral* and several popular TV series, including *Blackadder,* studied English at Christ Church.

Scholars and Teachers

Christ Church's dual role as college and cathedral has encouraged a distinctive tradition of academic excellence and scholarship. Many Deans and Canons have been distinguished academics, not least Thomas Gaisford (1779-1855), Regius Professor of Greek and Dean of Christ Church from 1831, and Henry Chadwick (1920-2008), a noted church historian. Rowan Williams, the Archbishop of Canterbury, was a Canon and Professor during the 1980s. Foreign scholars have been welcomed over the centuries, and in 1931 Frederick Lindemann, Professor of Physics and later Churchill's wartime scientific adviser, arranged for Albert Einstein to be awarded a research fellowship. Safe from Nazi persecution, he was accommodated at Christ Church, 'the calm cloisters of which he relished as much as Oxford relished him', according to a historian of science.

Dr Rowan Williams (1950-), theologian and archbishop. ◑

Hugh Trevor-Roper (1914-2003), historian. ◑

Thomas Gaisford (1779-1855), classical scholar and Dean of Christ Church (1831-1855), by Henry William Pickersgill (1782-1875). ◑

Albert Einstein (1879-1955), physicist. ◑

Other alumni of Christ Church: a selection

W.H. Auden (1907-1973), *poet*
Alfred Ayer (1910-1989), *philosopher*
George Bell (1883-1958), *bishop*
Zulfikar Ali Bhutto (1928-1979), *Prime Minister of Pakistan*
William Buckland (1784-1856), *geologist*
Charles Canning (1812-1862), *Governor General of India*
David Dimbleby (b.1938), *broadcaster*
Geoffrey Faber (1889-1961), *publisher*
Michael Flanders (1922-1975), *actor and entertainer*
Lord Hailsham (1907-2001), *politician*
Roy Harrod (1900-1978), *economist*
Trevor Huddleston (1913-1998), *archbishop and anti-apartheid campaigner*
Marina Hyde (b.1974), *journalist*
Ludovic Kennedy (1919-2009), *broadcaster*
John Kidd (1775-1851), *scientist*
Nigel Lawson (b.1932), *politician*
John Locke (1632-1704), *philosopher*
Denis Mahon (1910-2011), *art historian*
Jan Morris (b.1926), *writer*
Edward Bouverie Pusey (1800-1882), *leader of the Oxford Movement*
A.L. Rowse (1903-1997), *historian*
Gilbert Ryle (1900-1976), *philosopher*
Jonny Searle (b.1969), *Olympic gold medallist*
Donald Swann (1923-1994), *musician and entertainer*
Hugh Trevor-Roper (1914-2003), *historian*
Peter Warlock (1894-1930), *composer*
Auberon Waugh (1939-2001), *writer*
John Wesley (1703-1791), *founder of Methodism*

British Prime Ministers:

George Grenville (1712–1770)
Earl of Shelburne (1737–1805)
Duke of Portland (1738–1809)
Lord Grenville (1759–1834)
Earl of Liverpool (1770–1828)
George Canning (1770 1827)
Sir Robert Peel (1788–1850)
Earl of Derby (1799–1869)
William Ewart Gladstone (1809–1898)
Marquess of Salisbury (1830–1903)
Earl of Rosebery (1847–1929)
Sir Anthony Eden (1897–1977)
Sir Alec Douglas-Home (1903–1995)

Clockwise from right: Farmer Charlie Gee with his excellent strawberry crop at Medley Manor Farm, Binsey;

Meadows and cottages in Binsey Village;

The Perch at Binsey, a much loved destination for diners and walkers on Port Meadow;

Some American Friends of Christ Church;

The parish church at Iffley, one of a number of Christ Church 'livings'.

Finances and development

Christ Church's unique joint foundation of both college and cathedral, the grandeur of the architecture, and the sheer size of the curtilage all add greatly to its financial responsibilities. It must maintain not just the college's infra-structure and educational activities, but also the cathedral, the Cathedral School, the Picture Gallery and the Meadow.

In large part it has been able to do this because of its endowment—gifts that have been donated over the years. Christ Church also has its own income-generating operations, such as conferences and tourism, which bring in over 15% of total income, so thank you for visiting!

Of greatest importance, however, has been the generosity of individuals who since the time of Cardinal Wolsey and King Henry VIII have added to the college's endowment, allowing it to plan ahead with confidence.

About 45% of annual income is derived from the endowment, which is invested about one third each in property, equities, and diversified investments. Christ Church owns over 4,000 hectares of land mostly in Oxfordshire and neighbouring counties, which it rents to farmers. It also owns one of Oxford's most popular pubs, The Perch at Binsey. Its financial assets are overseen by the Treasurer and a group of advisors, but most investment is undertaken by Oxford University Endowment Management and by Oxford Investment Partners (OXIP), established in 2006 at the initiative of Christ Church to look after investments for five Oxford colleges.

Christ Church's running costs are more than most other colleges because of its size and history; some 20% of annual expenditure goes on such infrastructure costs. Furthermore about £3 million a year has to be found for the restoration and upgrading of the historic buildings. Direct academic and student costs account for over 50% of expenditure, and the college subsidises the cost of each undergraduate's education significantly from its own resources – a fact not always sufficiently recognised.

Thus, despite the institution's large endowment and income, the scale of its costs has meant that it has generally been left with a funding gap. This is why bequests and other donations are vitally important to ensure that Christ Church can maintain its standards and fulfil its aims and objectives. In 2008 Michael Moritz, an undergraduate from 1973, and his wife Harriet Heyman, gave a landmark donation of £25 million. This sum, together with significant gifts from the Oppenheimer family and other alumni, has allowed Christ Church to undertake important restoration work, endow academic posts, and boost endowment income, taking the institution closer to financial independence and an assured future.

In addition to fund-raising, the Christ Church Development & Alumni Office works with the Christ Church Association and the American Friends of Christ Church to maintain close relations with the members of the college, to help keep them in touch with each other and with the institution, and to establish a life-long commitment with them to safeguard the traditions and values of Christ Church in perpetuity.

Michael Moritz and Harriet Heyman.

Nicky Oppenheimer.

Cathedral events

The cathedral is primarily a place of worship and reflection, welcoming thousands of people each week into its atmosphere of peace and mystery. But as well as being a working church and chapel it is also a place where all sorts of artistic and cultural events take place, ranging from dance and concerts to lectures and exhibitions.

The cathedral's calendar follows that of the Church of England, with special services marking the important Christian seasons and festivals. Christmas, in particular, is a treasured moment in the cathedral's year, as carol services featuring the Cathedral Choir are enormously popular among people from Oxford and further afield. Services are sometimes broadcast on radio, and recordings of the Cathedral Choir are available from the gift shop. The feast day of St Frideswide is also celebrated in mid October.

Sound checking for a performance. ↷

Orchestra and Cathedral Choir in performance. ↷↷

Clockwise ↻:
Roly Bain, priest/clown;
Candlemas Carols;
Rambert School dancers;
Palm Sunday procession.

The cathedral keeps long hours, and there are services each day. Morning prayer is held at 7.15am daily, followed by Holy Communion, while Evensong takes place at 6pm. In between, the cathedral choir practises and a stream of visitors, including many school parties, is welcomed by cathedral stewards and education staff who are happy to answer questions and give tours.

During Holy Week there are meditations and musical events, showcasing the cathedral organ as well as the choir. On certain Sundays, the popular and informal After Eight service brings together people from many different backgrounds to discuss matters of faith and spirituality. There are also the annual summer lectures, where speakers explore a wide range of issues.

The cathedral's exceptional acoustics and range of spaces make it an exciting place for live performances of all sorts. Recent events have included piano concertos, orchestral concerts and dance performances from the members of the Rambert School of Ballet and Contemporary Dance, with which the cathedral has established close links. Perhaps most appropriate was the Oxford Playhouse's production of T. S. Eliot's *Murder in the Cathedral*, the re-enactment of the last days of Archbishop Thomas Becket, where the atmosphere perfectly matched the unfolding drama.

Hospitality and events

For three ten-week periods each year Christ Church is busy with the work of an Oxford teaching term. Outside the three terms, however, the college also opens its doors to a wide range of groups and organisations. The institution is committed to offering access to its unique facilities to as many different individuals and bodies as possible. It has the resources to host successful conferences, seminars and summer schools as well as organising its own events.

Boasting accommodation for up to 300 people, including 130 rooms with private shower and toilet facilities, Christ Church can also provide a 130-seat lecture theatre, several seminar and meeting rooms and state-of-the-art technology for presentations and lectures. Conference delegates enjoy access to the college gardens and Christ Church Meadow as well as the cathedral and Picture Gallery. Experienced college staff offer a level of professionalism that guarantees the success of any event.

The long-running and sought-after Oxford Experience summer programme of one-week courses enables participants to sample life at Christ Church while following a short but in-depth course of study. Over fifty topics, both in the arts and sciences, are available and are aimed at non-specialist students who are taught in small, informal seminar groups. Those attending the courses benefit from teaching modelled on the traditional Oxford tutorial system while enjoying their stay in the college's comfortable and modernised accommodation.

Christ Church also organises and hosts occasional special interest weekends, centred

Beautiful lunches... ↻

...inspiring menus... ↻

...exquisite settings. ↻

on specific topics of academic interest. Like the week-long courses, these are of particular interest to non-specialists and involve staying in one of the college's rooms and dining in Hall.

Each year in spring the college hosts the Oxford Literary Festival, a hugely popular gathering of writers, readers and book-lovers. Thousands of literature enthusiasts from around the world converge on Christ Church for a feast of talks, workshops and other events. With an ever-growing roll-call of international and British authors, the festival combines the best of contemporary literature with the timeless appeal of Christ Church and the wider University. Talks and other events are staged in many parts of the college, while a marquee facing the Meadow houses a bookshop and café.

Dr Peter McDonald (second from left), Christ Church's Christopher Tower Tutor in Poetry, with three young writers who have been associated with Tower Poetry: Alex Bell, Olivia Cole and Nick Pierpan, at a Tower Poetry event at Christ Church. (See page 69).

Charity cyclists arriving from London.

Philosopher Peter Singer, at a conference on his work organised by the McDonald Centre for Theology, Ethics & Public Life, which is based at Christ Church.

The wonder of Alice lives on in children's events.

Tourism

Christ Church is primarily an educational and religious institution, but it is by no means a closed community and welcomes visitors from all over the world who wish to see its unique architecture and peaceful Meadow. While visitors are encouraged to enjoy its sights and atmosphere, it is also expected that they respect its working and spiritual environment.

Visitors play a vital role in maintaining the fabric of Christ Church's buildings and grounds, their admission fees helping to finance repairs and refurbishment and support the cost of a large professional staff of gardeners and Custodians. Christ Church is open almost all year round, but is particularly busy in the summer months. Approximately 300,000 individuals visit each year and Christ Church has been ranked number one among Oxford's tourist attractions.

As well as the walking tour that takes visitors through the Cloister, the cathedral, the Hall and main quadrangles, there is also the opportunity to visit the Picture Gallery with its important collection of Renaissance art (a small extra entrance fee is payable) and there are occasional enhanced 'Behind the Scenes' tours that include gardens and other aspects of the college.

Schoolchildren learn about the role of a bishop on educational visits. ↷↷

Visitors of all ages enjoy the chance to experience Christ Church's unique place in centuries of history. ↷↶

Christ Church's famous 'Custodians' make everyone welcome and ensure that visiting and learning can take place together. ↷↷

54

Behind the scenes

4

The gardens

The gardens may at first sight appear to be as old and venerable as some of the buildings but most are in fact relatively recent, dating from the 19th and 20th centuries. Before then Christ Church was bounded on its south and east sides by the Meadow and to the north and west by streets. Space within the walls was given up mostly to stores and outbuildings, and the only gardens of any importance were those attached to the Deanery and Canonries. The huge expanse of Tom Quad lacked – and still does – any sign of gardening apart from its lawns, and the same applies to Peckwater Quad. Only one tree can confidently be described as ancient.

This was to change from the 1860s onwards, and slowly a succession of open spaces was cleared and planted, leading from the Memorial

Memorial Garden gate. ⌂

The Memorial Garden greets visitors from St Aldates with a beautiful view of the Hall and 'Auden Cottage', where the poet W.H. Auden lived. ⌂

Garden (1926), around the Meadow Building to the Masters' Garden and then through the Pocock Garden to the centre of the college.

The Masters' Garden is open to all members of the college. From here there is a superb view of Merton College and more distant Magdalen, with a section of the old city wall separating the garden from Deadman's Walk. A huge lawn is much used in the summer months, while around are mixed herbaceous borders and yews.

A gate leads into the nearby Pocock Garden. Above its walls, you can see the celebrated Oriental plane tree planted by Edward Pocock, Professor of Arabic, in the mid-17th century. This gnarled veteran, grown from seed brought back from the Middle East, is thought to have inspired Lewis Carroll's poem on the Jabberwock in *Through the Looking Glass* – though there is little evidence.

Further, more reliable echoes of Dodgson and Alice are to be found in the Cathedral Garth where Dean Liddell, Alice's father, is buried together with his wife Lorina and daughter Edith. Alice would have played in the Deanery Garden, separated from the Cathedral Garden by a wall. A small door in this wall is thought to be the 'magic door' to Wonderland. Also in the Deanery Garden is a large chestnut tree in which the Cheshire Cat sat and grinned – and vanished.

Another door takes us further back, to the Civil War when Charles I was accommodated in the Deanery. His wife Henrietta Maria and her children and retinue were housed in nearby Merton, and so Charles demanded – and duly received – a 'royal shortcut' in the form of a small door through the wall between Christ Church and Corpus Christi.

Alice's gate, from the Deanery Garden to the Cathedral Garden. ⌂

The Masters' Garden borders. ⌂⌂

Watering cans in the Orangery. ⌂
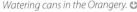

Tom Tower

Tom Tower is perhaps Christ Church's most distinctive and visible architectural feature, but it was something of an afterthought. We do not know whether Cardinal Wolsey intended a tower of some sort on his gatehouse, but when he died it was no taller than the rest of the quadrangle. Christ Church had to wait until 1681 and Dean John Fell's vigorous construction programme for Christopher Wren to submit his design for a new tower. By the end of the following year Tom Tower was finished.

Wren's design is Gothic, intended to complement the earlier gatehouse and façade and to avoid what he called 'an unhandsome medley'. But the architect also added some more unconventional features of his own, including the two turrets on the street side. Niches were provided for statues, and Cardinal Wolsey finally found himself looking over St Aldates in 1872 whereas Queen Anne surveys the quadrangle. Legend has it that Wren never returned to Oxford to inspect his finished work.

Great Tom, the bell that gives the Tower and Quad their name, had its origins in the medieval Osney Abbey and was then brought to hang in the cathedral's spire before being moved across the quadrangle to its present location. Over the centuries it has been recast seven times to preserve its deep, sonorous tone. It is the loudest bell in Oxford and also the heaviest, which has meant that it has had to be re-hung several times, most recently in 1953.

Apart from a period during the Second World War, Great Tom has rung the hour (now only during the daytime) since 1684. It also tolls 101 times starting at 9.05pm. The first number commemorates the original one hundred scholars of the college, plus an additional one added by bequest. The five-minute delay after 9.00pm is due to 'Oxford time' or local mean time, which is five minutes later than Greenwich. In Dean Fell's day the ringing of Tom Bell signalled a curfew and stray undergraduates were meant to return quickly to college.

Tom Tower is off-limits to visitors, but a winding wooden 111-step staircase still leads up to the gallery in which Great Tom hangs. Nowadays the bell normally rings mechanically but it was once the job of college staff to ring the 101 chimes. By tradition it falls silent for the funeral of a Dean and it was also silenced in 1965 at the death of Sir Winston Churchill.

Great Tom hangs in the Tower which bears its name. ⬆

John Riley's 1680s painting 'A Scullion of Christ Church' depicts the recently completed Tom Tower. ⬇

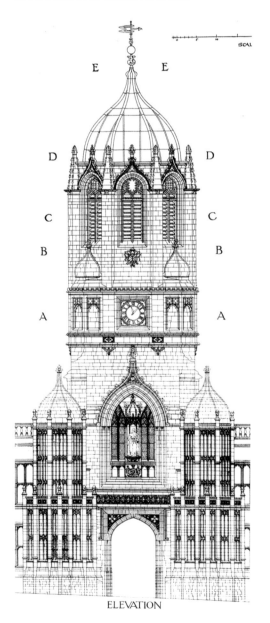

ELEVATION

The staircase inside the Tower bears the evidence of many visitors in the past. ⬆

The east side of Tom Tower faces the Quadrangle and is decorated with a statue of Queen Anne, dating from 1712. ◉

Upper Library

During the protracted process of building the Library (1717-72) the upper storey of the building remained more consistent in its planned form than did the lower storey, which was modified from an open loggia to two separate rooms. The Upper Library was intended to hold valuable books, as it was less at risk from damp and flooding. From the outset, though, it seemed that it would struggle to contain the large numbers of books and other documents bequeathed by benefactors. As early as the 1750s a gallery was constructed to hold the collection of Charles Boyle, fourth Earl of Orrery, and at the same time four windows were concealed by additional bookcases to house further donations.

In 1752 the plasterwork decoration of the Upper Library's ceiling was undertaken by a local craftsman by the name of Thomas Roberts. His ornate cream and gold handiwork can be admired from outside the Library. Most of the upper storey's interior and fittings are from the mid-18th century and include stools made by the master furniture designer, Thomas Chippendale. At this time the building was heated only by wrought-iron braziers in which charcoal was burnt.

The scale of the Upper Library – it is nearly 150 feet in length – allows it to hold an impressive 40,000 volumes. These are normally arranged according to the name of the donor. In total, there are some 100,000 early printed books, making the library the sixth largest holder of such volumes in the UK. Cataloguing and conservation is a large and on-going task, contributing significantly to manuscript and historical research. The Upper Library is closed to visitors, but scholars from around the world are able, by special appointment, to consult its books and manuscripts.

The oldest work in the collection is a late 8th-century monk's chronicle, hand-written in Greek. There are also several hundred medieval manuscripts and over 100 incunabula – books printed before 1501, the oldest of which dates from 1468. One of the most important bequests was made by William Wake, Archbishop of Canterbury from 1716 to 1737. His collection included printed books, Greek manuscripts and rare coins, which were subsequently transferred to the Ashmolean Museum.

Charles Dodgson was a sub-librarian here, and from the library windows looking down over the Deanery garden he may have first noticed Alice and the other Liddell children.

The Upper Library was beautifully restored in 2010 and is used for exhibitions of books, manuscripts and artefacts.

Early printed books of world class importance also give insight into Christ Church in the past.

Special Interest Weekend guests learn about Civil War armour in the Upper library. ⊙⊙

The Roman statue of Eros and Aphrodite, bequeathed to Christ Church in 1805. ⊙

59

The kitchen

The huge kitchen, dating from 1526, and the accompanying Buttery and Cellars were among the first facilities installed by Cardinal Wolsey. As with the Hall and main quadrangle, he planned on a massive scale, and the kitchen is an impressive forty feet square and sixty feet high. Even today, after considerable modernisation and refurbishment, the room's scale is breathtaking, and much remains of its original design and character.

In Wolsey's day the kitchen boasted three large fireplaces, each with its own chimney, which were used for roasting meat. Up to forty legs of mutton or seventy chickens could be cooked on revolving spits that were powered by an ingenious convection heating system. Any smoke or steam that was not drawn up into the chimneys escaped though a central ventilation lantern, which is still in place. Also surviving is a large basin used for crushing the herbs and spices that were essential for making sauces. A separate part of the room was devoted to baking.

The kitchen retains many other ancient features, including locks on a now-closed window that were deployed every night to prevent hungry undergraduates from breaking in and helping themselves to the contents of the Kitchen. Large mullion windows also date from Wolsey's period. Outside, by the enclosed staircase leading to the Hall, is a small counter where a clerk would have sat checking that the food was not intercepted on its way to the college members.

An echo of *Alice's Adventures in Wonderland* is to be found in the form of two turtle shells hanging on a wall. These were apparently used to make turtle soup for the Prince of Wales (later King Edward VII) and may have inspired Lewis Carroll's imaginative creation, the Mock Turtle – the name of a soup that does not in fact include the edible reptile.

Nowadays the kitchen is rarely quiet, producing over 200,000 meals each year for the academic community, conferences and special events. Recent refurbishment has included state-of-the-art ovens and refrigeration, including ranges designed in an appropriately vivid cardinal red. A head chef leads a team of seventeen chefs and apprentices, ensuring that Christ Church's tradition of hospitality is maintained in one of Britain's oldest kitchens.

A painting of the kitchen by Augustus Charles Pugin, reproduced in Ackerman's 'History of Oxford' in 1814. ◑

Ancient turtle shells hang above one of the kitchen fireplaces, reminders of 18th-century banquets, and the stories of Lewis Carroll. ◑

Fine wines from Christ Church's cellars can accompany outstanding cuisine. ◐

Lunch preparation in Wolsey's Kitchen. ◑

Dining in style. ⬆

Executive Head Chef, Chris Simms. ⬅

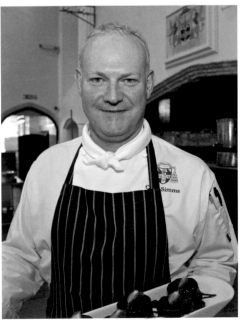

Ancient copper pans still decorate a fireplace in today's efficient working kitchen. ➡

The Senior Common Room

The Senior Common Room is where senior members – and their guests – congregate before and after dinner and at other times of the day. There are in fact several rooms, some of them also used for events and meetings. The much older part of it is to be found across the Schools Quadrangle in a comfortable room below the Dining Hall. This dates from a 1667 benefaction by Dr Busby, headmaster of Westminster School, who left money so that this room could be used for lectures and for 'the use of the Masters for their Publick fires'. Appropriately, a bust of Dr Busby now stands above the common room's open fire. Other figures commemorated in this room include the philosopher John Locke, who was a Student in the mid-1660s. There are portraits, too, of the 13 British prime ministers from Christ Church and of nine viceroys of India. Senior members gather here, in what is known as the Old Common Room, before dinner during term. A stone spiral staircase leads those dining in Hall up to the entrance at the side of High Table. The High Table does not function during the vacations, when those wishing to dine can do so in less formal surroundings.

Across the Schools quadrangle is the other area used by the members of the Senior Common Room, a compact Georgian house, now known as the Lee Building. This was built in 1767 with money donated by Matthew Lee, a former college undergraduate who was physician to Frederick, Prince of Wales. For over a century the building was the scene of grisly dissections, being used by the University's Anatomy School. At that time it contained a lecture theatre with a gallery containing specimens around it, while below, according to records, was a laboratory used for dissecting human cadavers. These were delivered via a back door from the Meadow, and there was even reputedly a large receptacle with a stream running through it in which body parts could be thrown away. The Senior Common Room expanded into the Lee Building as recently as the 1970s. The former lecture theatre is now used as the senior members' lunch room and is also the setting for meetings of the Governing Body (the council of academics and clergy which governs Christ Church) and occasional private functions. As for the basement, it currently houses a bar for undergraduate use.

Tutors, Lecturers and Research Fellows relax and discuss college business in the Senior Common Room. ◉◉◉

Victorian firescreen with mythical beasts depicted in tiles by William de Morgan. ◉

Blue Boar Quad

The popular image of Christ Church is of Tom Quad with its Tudor-era formality or the medieval cloister, but there is also a modern aspect to the college's architectural heritage, most notably in the picture gallery and in Blue Boar Quadrangle.

Blue Boar is named after a medieval inn that was on the north side of the college wall. In the early twentieth century Blue Boar was the site of a bath house for undergraduates. Until the 1960s the area in question was also a real tennis court and then accommodation for Canons, before becoming a coal yard and an undistinguished collection of car parks and garages. It was finally cleared to make way for the plans of the architectural firm of Powell & Moya (who also designed the Picture Gallery). Work began in 1965 and was completed three years later. Comprising accommodation for undergraduates and larger penthouses occupied by senior members and used for teaching, the complex answered a need for more student rooms at a time when the college – and Oxford University as a whole – was fast expanding.

Blue Boar is constructed from a mixture of stones, with an emphasis on maximising light through large windows. The modest and practical nature of the complex has earned it plaudits, and in 2006 it became a Grade II* listed building as, in the words of the Minister of Culture, 'one of the best buildings of its kind during the expansion of higher education'. Others are less keen on what is seen as a plain and utilitarian architectural style, but Blue Boar allowed a considerable amount of accommodation to be discreetly fitted into a small and unused space.

A recent renovation programme has retained its 1960s openwork character, and added a lecture theatre and exhibition space as well as modernising 79 bedrooms. These, in term time, normally accommodate first-year undergraduates and the rest of the year are used by participants at conferences and other events.

Not everything is modern in this part of the college. The Archives are stored in a brewhouse believed to be 16th-century in origin. They were moved out of Blue Boar during the renovation to make room for the new lecture theatre.

Prospective students discuss their Open Day experience in Blue Boar's amphitheatre.

A perfect place to study too.

Blue Boar Quad. ⬆

The new lecture theatre
is in constant use for
conferences and
teaching. ◗

5   Christy Church and the imagination

Lewis Carroll and Alice

Two of the most enduring works of English literature owe their inspiration to Christ Church and to the creativity of a man who spent all of his adult life at the college. *Alice's Adventures in Wonderland* and *Through the Looking Glass* were written by Lewis Carroll, the pen-name of Charles Lutwidge Dodgson (1832-98). Dodgson came to Christ Church as an undergraduate in 1851 and was an exceptional mathematician, winning a college Lectureship. He taught mathematics and in 1861 was ordained Deacon, although he never became a priest.

Interested in the early art of photography, Dodgson was also fascinated by story-telling. His imaginative gifts came to light in 1856 when the family of Dean Henry Liddell moved into the college. The Dean's children included the young Alice Liddell, who was drawn to the shy young don. He, in return, struck up a friendship with all the Liddell children, taking them on walks in Christ Church Meadow and boating trips on the Thames. In the summer of 1862 Dodgson and the children rowed up the river to the small hamlet of Godstow for a picnic. During the excursion Dodgson continued to develop the fantastic stories that he had told them, featuring himself, Alice's sisters Edith and Lorina and, of course, Alice herself.

"It was much pleasanter at home, when one wasn't always growing larger and smaller, and being ordered about by mice and rabbits."

Charles Dodgson by Oscar Gustave Rejlander, 1863. ⤴

Alice's gate to the Cathedral Garden in the snow. ⤴

Hall windows commemorate Alice Liddell and Charles Dodgson with illustrations from the stories. ⤵

The Jabberwock as depicted by John Tenniel. ⤵

The majestic Oriental Plane tree in the Pocock Garden is thought to be the inspiration for the Jabberwock. ⤵

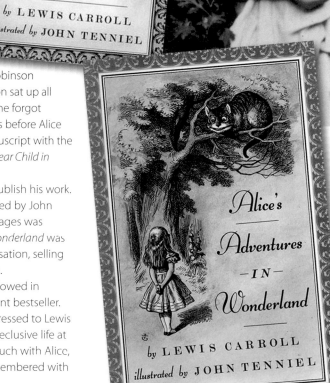

Normally, recalled Dodgson, his tales 'lived and died like summer midges', but this time it was to be different. When they returned to the college, Alice begged Dodgson to write down 'her' adventures. His friend, the Rev Robinson Duckworth, recalled that Dodgson sat up all night scribbling his ideas before he forgot them. But it was to take two years before Alice was given the hand-written manuscript with the inscription *'A Christmas Gift to a Dear Child in Memory of a Summer Day'*.

Friends urged Dodgson to publish his work. With the illustrations later provided by John Tenniel, the mix of words and images was complete. *Alice's Adventures in Wonderland* was published in 1865 and was a sensation, selling hundreds of thousands of copies.

Through the Looking Glass followed in 1871, but Dodgson was a reluctant bestseller. He refused to answer letters addressed to Lewis Carroll and lived a quiet, almost reclusive life at Christ Church. He remained in touch with Alice, however, and until his death remembered with fondness the 'golden afternoon'.

Alice Liddell as a street urchin in a photograph by Charles Dodgson. ⬆

First edition book covers. ↩

Alice, from a set of carved figures in the Upper Library. ↩

The Queen of Hearts, reputedly modelled on Alice's governess who lived at Binsey. ↩

"You're nothing but a pack of cards!" An illustration by John Tenniel. ↓

ROYAL
OPERA
HOUSE

Literature and filming

Lovers of Lewis Carroll and his imaginary world find much of interest in the college where he spent his entire adult life, ranging from scenes and objects that inspired him to clues about his fictional characters. Visitors can see for themselves the place where Alice and her siblings were brought up and where Charles Dodgson created his much-loved masterpieces. The Meadow and river remain much as they were during that period, and several sites in the college itself are believed to appear – in imagined form – in his writing.

Christ Church has fired the imagination of others. Harking back to its 16th-century origins, Cardinal College features in Thomas Hardy's novel *Jude the Obscure,* where Oxford is portrayed as Christminster. Cardinal College also appears in the 1938 film *A Yank in Oxford* starring Vivien Leigh and Robert Taylor, lampooned by Laurel and Hardy in 1940 in *A Chump at Oxford.*

More recently, the phenomenon of Harry Potter has brought parts of Christ Church – the Cloister, the Hall Stairs and the Hall – onto the silver screen, with the Hall acting as the inspiration for a recreated Hogwarts Hall. Christ Church has also appeared in episodes of the popular television series *Inspector Morse* and

© ITV/Rex Features

Lewis as well as in *The Golden Compass,* a film based on the novel by Oxford author Philip Pullman. All of these locations are freely accessible to visitors who wish to see for themselves where Professor McGonagall greeted the Hogwarts students or where Lewis Carroll invented the world of Alice.

With its associations with the great Elizabethan poet Sir Philip Sidney and more recently W.H. Auden, it is appropriate that Christ Church is the home of Tower Poetry, which aims to stimulate an enjoyment and critical appreciation of poetry, particularly among young people. Activities include a summer school for young poets, and the Christopher Tower Poetry Prize, which is open to any UK student aged 16 to 18.

Promotional poster for the the Royal Ballet's 2011 production of 'Alice in Wonderland' featuring Lauren Cuthbertson (and Julie, the Deanery cat).

John Thaw and Kevin Whately. Several episodes of 'Morse' and 'Lewis' have been filmed at Christ Church.

Dumbledore, headmaster of Hogwarts.

Photograph by Jason Bell – © Royal Opera House

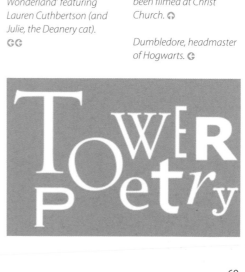

Christ Church in words...

I surveyed the chiefest colleges. 1st Christ-church, which was meant to have been a famous monument, but never finished by the Founder, Cardinal Wolsey: it was meant to be a square of 8 score: three parts built, but the church not builded: there I saw the fairest hall with great church windows, and the largest kitchen I ever saw.
Sir Roger Wilbraham, Diary, 1603

The beautiful meadows lay green and bright in the sun; the arching trees threw a softened light, and made a chequered pavement of the great Broad Walk; 'witch-elms *did* counter-change the floor' of the gravel-walks that wound with the windings of the Cherwell; the drooping willows were mirrored in its stream; through openings in the trees there were glimpses of grey old college-buildings; then came the walk along the banks, the Isis shining like molten silver, and fringed around with barges and boats; then another stretch of green meadows; then a cloud of steam from the railway-station; and a background of gently rising hills.
Cuthbert Bede, *Adventures of Mr Verdant Green*, 1853

I walked along, thro' the lovely Christ Church meadow, by the river side and back through the town. It was a perfect evening and in the interminable British twilight the beauty of the whole place came forth with magical power. There are no words for these colleges.
Henry James, letter to William James, 1869

The cathedral itself was an epitome of English history. Every stone, every pane of glass, every panel of woodwork, was true, and of its time,—not an accused sham of architect's job. The first shrine of St. Frideswide had indeed been destroyed, and her body rent and scattered on the dust by the Puritan; but her second shrine was still beautiful in its kind,—most lovely English work both of heart and hand... The roof was true Tudor,—grotesque, inventively constructive, delicately carved; it, with the roof of the hall staircase, summing the builder's skill of the 15th century.
John Ruskin, *Praeterita*, 1885

There is a gentle and puissant harmonising influence in Oxford which nothing can escape. I am no lover of Georgian architecture and am often blind to the power of Wren; but in Oxford I have no such incapacities... The library at Christ Church, or any other work of the 18th century, seems to be as

divine a thing, though as yet it lacks the complete unction of antiquity, as Mob Quad at Merton or Magdalen Tower. To pass from the Norman work of St. Peter's in the East to the Palladianism of Peckwater quadrangle, is but to descend from one to another of the same honourable race.
Edward Thomas, *Oxford*, 1903

These singular results achieved at Oxford are all the more surprising when one considers the distressing conditions under which the students work. The lack of an adequate building fund compels them to go on working in the same old buildings which they have had for centuries… At Christ Church I was shown a kitchen which had been built at the expense of Cardinal Wolsey in 1527. Incredible though it may seem, they have no other place to cook in than this and are compelled to use it today.
Stephen Leacock, *My Discovery of England,* 1922

I consider my membership of Christ Church one of the most precious gifts to have been bestowed on me and I do not imagine that without early access to its balance of vision, tolerance and understanding I would have proceeded in life with quite so much fulfilment, not to mention pleasure.
David Hughes, letter to the Dean, 2004

Further reading and resources

ON OXFORD
John Dougill, *Oxford in English Literature.* Oxface, 2010
Christopher Hibbert (ed.), *The Encyclopaedia of Oxford.* Macmillan, 1992
Insight City Guide: Oxford. APA, 2006
Jan Morris, *Oxford.* Oxford University Press, 3rd edn., 2001
Jan Morris (ed.), *The Oxford Book of Oxford.* Oxford University Press, 2002
Jennifer Sherwood and Nikolaus Pevsner, *The Buildings of England: Oxfordshire.* Yale University Press, 1974
Edward Thomas, *Oxford* (1903). Signal Books, 2005
Geoffrey Tyack, *Oxford: An Architectural Guide.* Oxford University Press, 1998
A. R. Woolley, *The Clarendon Guide to Oxford.* Oxford University Press, 1963

On Christ Church
E. G. W. Bill, *Education at Christ Church 1660-1800.* Oxford University Press, 1988
E. G. W. Bill and J. F. A. Mason, *Christ Church and Reform.* Oxford University Press, 1970
Christopher Butler (ed.), *Christ Church, Oxford: A Portrait of the House.* Third Millennium Publishing, 2006
Christ Church Picture Gallery, Oxford. Christ Church Picture Gallery, 2002
Judith Curthoys, *The Cardinal's College: Christ Church, Chapter and Verse.* Profile Books, 2012
P. W. Kent, *Some Scientists in the Life of Christ Church, Oxford.* Christ Church, 2001
J. Thalmann (ed) *Forty years of Christ Church Picture Gallery.* Oxford 2008
H. R. Trevor-Roper, *Christ Church, Oxford: The Portrait of a College.* Christ Church, 1950, 3rd edn., 1989

Many of these publications, as well as a wider range of books and gifts, are available from the Cathedral Shop, situated in the cathedral cloisters.

Further information on Christ Church's history and current news, including cathedral services and events, can be found on www.chch.ox.ac.uk